Crawley
New Town

IN OLD PHOTOGRAPHS

Portnall Road, Paddington, celebrates peace in 1945. Dreams of a better life for the children, and the expectation that the government would look after the nation in peacetime, encouraged families to leave old neighbourhoods. Thousands of Londoners made a new life in Crawley from 1950.

Crawley New Town

IN OLD PHOTOGRAPHS

Collected by JEFFREY GREEN
and PETER ALLEN

Alan Sutton Publishing Limited
Phoenix Mill · Far Thrupp
Stroud · Gloucestershire

First published in 1993

Copyright © Jeffrey Green and Peter Allen 1993

British Library Cataloguing in Publication Data

Green, Jeffrey
Crawley New Town in Old Photographs
I. Title II. Allen, Peter
942.261

ISBN 0-7509-0472-0

Typeset in 9/10 Sabon.
Typesetting and origination by
Alan Sutton Publishing Limited.
Printed in Great Britain by
Redwood Books, Trowbridge.

Contents

Introduction   7

1. Beginning 1948–50   17

2. Brand New Homes   21

3. Employment   45

4. Rent Strike   71

5. Shopping   77

6. Carnival   95

7. Leisure   105

8. Sports and Games   119

9. Youngsters   127

10. People   143

11. Gatwick Airport   155

    Acknowledgements   160

Introduction

In October 1946 the Minister of Town and Country Planning, Lewis Silkin, told the London County Council that it could not build the cottage estate planned on 800 acres at Chessington. The LCC had allocated £475,000 for this – a vast sum at that time – expecting to house 20,000 people there. Silkin's letter stated that he hoped to 'make an effective start in building at Crawley within the next two or three years'. The minister and his Labour government colleagues had decided that London should no longer spew suburbs across farmland. People and factories would relocate to new towns, self-sufficient and complete communities of 50,000. Industries would have new factories, families would have new homes: the nation would have a new future.

Crawley, midway between London and the Channel coast, had 6,000 inhabitants in 1946. National and local government bodies had been considering what to do with Crawley for years, with West Sussex and East Sussex County Councils expressing concern over the urban sprawl between Crawley and, across the county boundary, Three Bridges. Rejecting two south of London proposals in the *Abercrombie Report*, the Ministry noted that Horsham could expand from 13,500 to 43,500, East Grinstead from 10,000 to 26,000, and Tonbridge from 16,000 to 30,000. The largest expansion would be 'a twin-centred town at Crawley-Three Bridges' tidying up the 'existing sprawl in that area to an eventual population of from 30,000 to 40,000'.

The report circulated within the ministries. The Board of Education indicated that 60,000 inhabitants would be required if secondary schools and colleges were to thrive in the New Town. Government file HLG 91/154 also reveals that officers from both county councils had conferred in April 1944, and had decided in June of that year to merge Three Bridges and Crawley into one town.

In 1946 the New Towns Bill went before parliament. At the second reading on 8 May Silkin stated that the need for new towns had been recognized in 1919 but nothing had been initiated. William Morrison, Conservative minister between 1940 and 1943, said the bill interfered with individual freedom and there were objections to compulsory purchase. On 10 July 1946 Silkin told parliament that Crawley would be one of the New Towns.

His ministry listed bodies to be invited to meet Silkin on 10 July. As the northern edge of Crawley New Town was in Surrey, three county councils were invited. Three rural district councils (RDCs) (Dorking and Horley, Cuckfield, and Horsham) and the London County Council were listed, but the LCC was struck off. That thousands of people and millions of pounds of industry were to be taken from London and relocated in Crawley New Town was not enough to keep the LCC on the list.

'Crawley really springs from local initiative and I very much hope that that

'A little country town', looking south-east, 1949. The large building (lower centre) is the cinema. Malthouse Road and the Brighton Road (top) disappear into farmland. West Green is to the right.

Crawley Development Corporation, 1949. Chaired by architect Thomas Bennett (centre) its unelected members were Mrs Douglas Bolton, Alderman J. Marshall, Lawrence Neal, Caroline Haslett, Ernest Stanford and E.W. Passold.

The Railway Hotel, *c.* 1959. Traditional jazz bands from London played in its dance hall. St Louis Jazz Club jivers met here on Wednesdays.

The Square, *c.* 1955. Traffic tries to enter Ifield Road. The police station kept a list of homes prepared to take lodgers. Getting a New Town job was the qualification for a Corporation home. Many took any job to qualify for a house.

Tinsley Lane, *c.* 1952. Nightingales and rabbits, bungalows and gardens made up the eastern side of the industrial estate. Bowthorpe restricted heavy presses because of the noise. The link road to the motorway was built here.

Woolworth's in the High Street (right). Princess Elizabeth planted a maple tree opposite in 1950, commemorating Canadian military links with Crawley between 1940 and 1945.

note will continue to be struck throughout its history,' was part of the draft speech for Silkin. He said nothing about rejecting the *Abercrombie Report* or the LCC's cottage estate plans. The reasons given were that the land was fairly level and the district's communications had east–west and north–south railways, an aerodrome, a planned new motorway, and a bypass. These elements would make the New Town a 'good distribution centre for industries based on the London market, industries connected with aero-engineering and maintenance and industries associated with the holiday trade of the South Coast towns'. This file, HLG 91/158 'Satellite Town Crawley-Three Bridges', states that Crawley was for 'people moved out of London', for the Sussex county councils could not nominate tenants.

Slum clearance and rehousing had been part of British life for years. Charities built flats in central London. London boroughs and the LCC built new homes. Private speculators put homes on the farms and market gardens of the Home Counties, linked by train to central London. Old market towns had become suburbs. Roads had 'ribbon development' as buses and cars became general. From palatial villas in Eastbourne to Peacehaven's huts, the town spread along the coast.

Crawley had expanded in the nineteenth century after the coming of the railway. Three Bridges was largely a railway settlement; homes had been built along its railway line in the 1930s and at Tinsley Lane near the grass aerodrome of Gatwick racecourse. To the west was Ifield Green. Between it and Crawley's main street was West Green, with Victorian and Horsham RDC houses.

Aggrieved people in Stevenage, Hemel Hempstead and Crawley took legal action against the declarations. Bad feeling stemmed from the powers to compulsorily purchase buildings and land given to the unelected development corporations. Crawley Development Corporation served notice to purchase over seventy properties, mainly in the High Street. Shopkeeper Daisy Warren expressed her views at the Railway Hotel enquiry in April 1949. 'We had our dreams for the future and you have smashed those dreams. You offer us a sum of money. Dreams are not bought with money, nor is their loss compensated by it.'

The invaders had dreams too. The dream was a home of their own. If your employer relocated to Crawley you qualified for a New Town home. Housing Office staff visited factories and homes to discuss house types and availability. Some firms arranged coach trips, and employees and families were shown finished homes and sites. Others came by train, by Greenline bus or motorcycle. Interviews were held at the Housing Office hut near Northgate Road. 'We could not have been treated better if we had been buying,' a Clapham man recalled. Mobile showrooms from the gas and electricity boards tempted migrants with cookers and heaters: 'We even bought our kettle on the never-never.' Salesmen from local dairies drove newcomers to look over possible homes, anticipating milk and grocery orders.

Rejecting suburbs and cottage estates the New Town planners expected the people to work locally. The industrial estate was placed so that pollution was blown away from the town, with two service industry areas near the railway. The Corporation selected a variety of employers from the hundreds requesting

The Brewery Shades. The off-licence (right) was merged into the pub. The shop (left) was to be the first Asian grocery in the New Town.

The High Street, looking south towards The Square and the level crossing, *c.* 1953.

information, avoiding a dominant employer or industry. However, Crawley did have an emphasis on electrical and other engineering.

Women workers were scarce. Bowthorpe had a Brighton factory by 1954 and Edwards employed women in Eastbourne. Twilight shifts were tried, with Stone employing twenty-five women from 6 to 10 p.m. in 1956. Vitamins Ltd had morning and afternoon shifts for women. The ambitions of New Towners led employers to speak of 'Crawley 'flu' (pregnancies).

Furnishing their own homes, raising a family and paying full rent often left little spare cash. High rents in Crawley were noted as early as 1952. In October 1955 there was a rent strike. Almost half the tenants rejected a rent increase.

It was hoped that migrants would bond into a new community, and neighbourhoods with shopping parades were built. The first, West Green, was close to the High Street shops. Northgate was east of the London Road's ribbon development, and had two homes turned into shops before its shopping parade was open. The Three Bridges neighbourhood had existing shops and pubs. Langley Green was far from the centre, as were later neighbourhoods.

The Tenants' Association and the Community Association were active. Five community huts were open by 1956, with Southgate's planned and Langley Green's being enlarged. Dances, meetings, social events, jumble sales, and events for children took place in the simple wooden huts, and through such activities newcomers made friends.

Large employers had their own sports and social clubs, which were most active at weekends and evenings. The cinema was very popular, as were dances. National youth groups expanded as the New Town grew. Trade unions had local representatives, and in 1959 during the strike at Universal Pattern & Precision Engineering Co. two shop stewards were served with writs, a new aspect of British labour relations. The Campaign for Nuclear Disarmament had a Crawley branch by 1958; so did the United Nations Assocation. Parents and teachers at Thomas Bennett School formed a singing group in 1958. Work continued on the theatre in an old barn in Ifield. Children were taken to the pantomime in London and Brighton, and had sports and other activities at schools.

The most public demonstration of the New Town's new spirit was the carnival, run by the Community Association from 1951. The large companies spent many hours preparing their floats, with friendly competition between Youngman, A.P.V., Stone, Longley and Jack Bowthorpe's companies. Bowthorpe and his cashier Johnny Dymock were stalwarts of the carnival committee. Thousands lined the streets and hundreds rode in the parades.

Crawley's new industries did not bring all their workers despite the lure of a brand new home. Labour shortages were reduced by Labour Exchanges and outer London boroughs notifying people with the required skills that Crawley would rehouse them if they obtained employment in the New Town.

Relocating a business could take years. Many New Towners had to travel back to London for months before their jobs relocated. There were problems adjusting to the life in Crawley. There are stories of women taking much of the pay packet on a Friday, scooping up the children and taking a train 'home' to

Daisy and Florrie Warren's hardware shop (left) was bought by the Development Corporation and leased back to the sisters. Anger and distress from compulsory purchases could have been avoided as many High Street buildings were in business forty years later.

Clearing the land for new homes. Coppice trees, farm buildings, military depots and machine-gun posts had to be cleared away before homes could be started.

London. Men often finished work at noon on Saturdays and then went to London to see a favourite soccer team or to meet old friends.

There were sports organizations in Crawley, with cricket long established in Ifield and Three Bridges, a soccer team, a revived rugby club, and company sports grounds. Staff at Vitamins Ltd made their own sports ground near Magpie Wood, which was rewarded by the director employing a professional groundsman. A.P.V. took over Jordans on the London Road, adding tennis courts and pitches. Many firms raised a soccer team.

Crawley Athletic Club and others welcomed the sports centre, which attracted future Olympic gold medallist Daley Thompson to the area. Boxing was important, and in Alan Minter the town had another international champion. The golf course was a financial and social success, which might have amused Thomas Bennett who opposed municipal socialism. It is believed that he rejected requests for a greyhound racing track.

The failure of the Health Authority to build a hospital on the allocated site (later Arden Road) is one example of how New Town plans could be ignored. It took time for the authorities to understand that Crawley was bursting with children, but the school building programme owed much to Councillor Norman Longley and his colleagues who gathered and printed details of the town's requirements, ensuring that schools were open at the right place and at the right time. West Green pioneers lacked proper schools.

Crawley College of Further Education, under Theodore Siklos, trained apprentices and workers for Crawley. The young people had enthusiasm, somehow aware of their parents' sacrifices and that new opportunities were there for them.

Some people associated with Crawley from the 1940s had taken opportunities that had led to fame. John George Haigh was famous in 1949 after the police discovered his acid bath in West Green had not destroyed the remains of one victim. Warrant Officer Sean Bourke of Ifield Air Training Corps later used his radio skills to spring Soviet spy George Blake from prison.

The national press also reported James Lee's protests. He had sold his farm to the Corporation before compensation was calculated on the value with permission to develop. Believing he had been swindled, 'Farmer' Lee's campaigning included driving a tractor to Buckingham Palace, which was shown on television. A quieter protest came from the elderly Mr Lanfear who did not want his smallholding at Magpie Wood taken by the Corporation and waved a gun (or an iron bar) at people approaching his land.

Others took opportunities after they moved to Crawley. Stella and Ron Heath produced braille books in their garden shed, expanding this service for the blind into full-time work. One Three Bridges youth migrated to California where he has success in music. Others took advantage of educational and vocational training, through apprenticeships, evening classes and college. Some drifted into drugs, some became police officers. Crawley New Town has its successes and its failures like any town.

'The explosives king of the New Town.' Reg Meadus (centre) had worked in Newfoundland forests and with explosives in the Army. With Tom 'Rusty' Langridge and up to forty men from Copthorne and Turners Hill, they used axes and blew up stumps to prepare sites for the New Town.

The Trustee Savings Bank (right), opened in July 1952. Thomas Bennett helped open new accounts. Factory workers did not have bank accounts in the 1950s.

SECTION ONE

Beginning 1948–50

The first New Town homes were started three years after Silkin's announcement. Much work had been done, with the men and women of the Crawley Development Corporation recruited and settled in offices at Broadfield House. Colonel Turner forged individuals with financial, accountancy, legal, administrative, design, architectural and engineering skills into a team. Plans were drawn up and costed. Bids were examined and contracts awarded. Land was purchased and cleared. Post-war Britain still had rationing, and imported materials including timber were scarce. Local people needed accommodation, but were outside the New Town's responsibilities, which led to bitterness until the rural district councils built more homes.

When the King's daughter visited Crawley in January 1950 to commemorate Canadian military links she was escorted over the bleak industrial estate by Silkin. Princess Elizabeth also met Old Town worthies, and building workers including Poles.

Princess Elizabeth and Lewis Silkin, 1950. The royal and ministerial visit in January could not conceal the empty land of the industrial estate, now named Manor Royal.

The King's daughter greets Crawley worthies, 1950.

Daisy Warren and Ernest Stanford, *c.* 1949. Miss Warren was bitter about the New Town. Stanford, charity worker and parish councillor, was enthusiastic that Sussex might have a Labour voice.

Waiting for the Princess in the High Street, 1950.

Crawley Development Corporation, late 1948.

See page 159 for names.

Brand New Homes

The planners thought they would attract a mixture of people by supplying homes to suit workers, management, and directors. Workers, the largest group (85 per cent), could have houses with between one and five bedrooms. From the start the New Town was different: not LCC-style slum clearance or low income housing, but a socially mixed community for people of all ages and classes. Bungalows were built for older people, and there were flats. At first these were let to young single people, but they had to be key workers in the new factories.

One quarter of West Green and Northgate homes were flats, but the Corporation was told that people wanted a house with a garden. The 1951 report notes that under 2 per cent of New Town migrants wanted flats. Crawley's clay made high-rise blocks expensive, but Bennett was opposed to flats and non-traditional homes despite pressure from the Conservative government which, from 1952, sought 300,000 new homes a year. In 1952 Crawley had fifty different housing types: two-thirds with three bedrooms and one quarter with two bedrooms. In 1955 concrete houses were built in Langley Green (152) and Northgate (142) but the Corporation refused high-rise and other modern buildings.

Smalls Mead was the first New Town street, built in 1949. Eleven companies put in bids for this prestigious contract. Hoad and Taylor's site managers were asked by the Development Corporation to keep the site neat and tidy for the 'hundreds of visitors' expected. Shortages of wood, delays with applications to the Ministry of Supply for materials, problems in housing the men who built the New Town's first homes, and a constant stream of visitors were some of the problems associated with this site. When the homes were ready it was discovered that there were no coal bunkers. One disgruntled worker bricked up the flue of a chimney as he built it, which was discovered after he left and cost a lot to put right.

Londoners on a day trip, mid-1950. Left to right: John Larner, John Lovett, Joe Chappell, Bert Wrench. This group, with cameraman Tony Leader, was taking a look at the town that would be home when Bale & Church relocated. Three had served in the Eighth Army. A fourth Army pal visited them in their new homes, and changed jobs to get a home in Crawley.

'Building workers' in West Green, 1950. A Saturday lunch-time in The George, combined with a zest for living, led the Bale & Church visitors to pose for this photograph.

New homes in Crawley, 1950. As an Essex woman recalled many saw their homes 'just two bricks high'. They would come by train every month or so: 'coming out of two rooms you would want to watch it going up'.

A washing-line of nappies. Dreams of a new home often included plans for a family. By 1956 nearly 90 per cent of New Town people were under 45 years old, and one thousand babies a year were expected.

Margaret Wragg the Housing Officer (left). She gave talks about the New Town in London factories, visited settlers in their new homes, and ran the Housing Office in a hut opposite Northgate Road. This photograph was taken in the winter of 1950/1.

A.P.V. visitors, late 1950. Workers, families and friends were taken to Crawley by A.P.V., the largest employer to move to the New Town. It had burst out of its original site in Wandsworth and had factories in Slough and White City. Within ten years A.P.V. employed one tenth of Crawley's industrial workers.

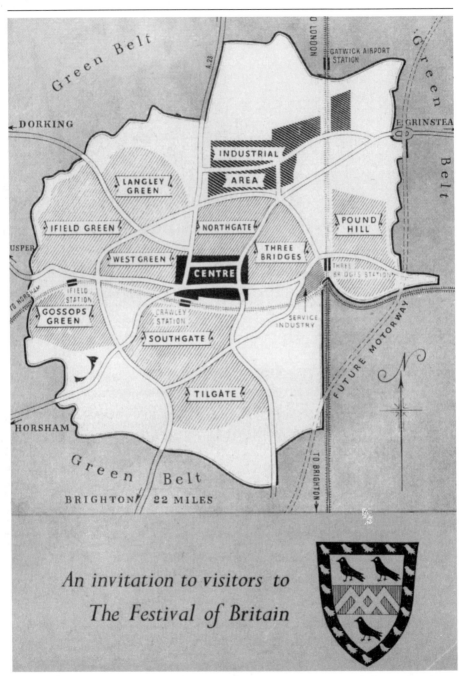

An invitation to visitors to

The Festival of Britain

London's Festival of Britain, 1951, proclaimed Crawley to be 'a balanced community planned to relieve London's congestion and spread'. Civic engineers were invited to see how sewers and pipes were laid under roadside verges, not the road, for easy access.

Three Bridges Road, *c.* 1957. Buses turning from the High Street had damaged the outfitters (left) but contractors demolished these shops which were purchased by the Development Corporation.

The High Street improved, *c.* 1958. Picturesque but shabby shops including a pawnbroker were compulsorily purchased by West Sussex County Council in the 1930s but the Corporation was blamed for demolishing The Square.

Punch Copse Road, *c.* 1957. When Les and Irene James moved here in 1953 they had to get used to cows looking over the back fence. Les James, in his pre-war Austin Seven, was one of the first car owners in the Three Bridges neighbourhood.

Gossops Green in winter, *c.* 1963. The mass of buildings in London had so much heat that snow seldom lasted. On the slopes of Gossops Green, winter snow and ice were fun for children but a hazard for those who cycled to work.

Ifield Park, 'a dilapidated Victorian mansion', 1993. The Goodwins found an old house for old people in a new town. Until it opened in 1954 couples were separated and sent to ex-workhouses in East Preston and Midhurst.

Harold and Millicent Goodwin, 1984. Their advertisement in *The Friend* led Bryan Richards of the Corporation to describe Ifield Park as above. By 1985 there were forty-six residents.

Northgate, *c.* 1955. Bricklayer Sid Ward had lived in ex-Army huts in Tilgate woods, then back in London, commuting to Crawley, until his family had a new home near his friend Wally; Wally's West Indian wife is seen here with Lorretta and Derek Ward.

The Embassy Cinema (far right). In 1954 seven hundred children attended every 'Saturday morning pictures' session. The cinema also opened on Sundays, although profits had to be shared with charities.

Buckmans Road, West Green, looking north, 1950. Dust from the sites, and cinders (because there were no pavements) covered the tile floors. A desolate atmosphere, not helped by the absence of street lights, was overcome in time.

West Green, 1950. Pavements came later in every neighbourhood. Mud and cinders were trodden in, so visitors brought slippers, and rubber boots stood outside every front door. Pioneers in each neighbourhood had to put up with thick mud on pram wheels and risked falling down holes in the dark.

Three Bridges neighbourhood, looking north, *c. 1956*. In the centre is St Richard's church. Builders are at work on the Maid of Sussex pub.

Heavy materials moved by railway in 1951. High Street traffic congestion was made worse as heavy and bulky loads were driven from Crawley station to West Green, Northgate, Langley Green and the factories.

Steel pipes for the water supply, 1951. Crawley station (left), looking towards Horsham. The sidings at Tinsley Lane were used for transporting coal.

Crawley's railway sidings, 1951. Land north of the new Crawley station was designated for sidings but motor transport triumphed. The Westminster Bank opened its administration office in Station Way in May 1963, an early non-industrial employer. Behind it, in Brunel Place, W. & T. Avery had their offices from 1967 until around 1990.

Honeysuckle Lane, Langley Green, *c.* 1953. It is believed one local businessman started a paving-stone factory and had a near-monopoly supplying the New Town.

Farm Close, Three Bridges, 1953. Plastering was the most time-consuming site task. A German plaster-throwing machine was examined and rejected, as smooth finishes were required.

Farm Close, Three Bridges. The excitement of seeing your new home nearing completion almost matched that of receiving the keys. Miss Wragg's team lent the keys of completed homes to future tenants who were able to look round thanks to local dairies whose salesmen drove them to the site from the Housing Office.

Placing homes around large trees and existing hedges took the raw edge off the New Town, and showed up the straight lines of Crawley's central shopping streets. One family found their back garden had been the lime-pit for builders, so the Corporation supplied two loads of top soil. A view with trees was appreciated.

Donne Close, Pound Hill, 1961. The idea that Crawley New Town would mainly offer rented homes vanished by the mid-1950s. Taylor Woodrow sold homes for £1,900 to £3,000, asking for a 10 per cent deposit.

Furnace Green did not appear on the first town plan, although in 1944 county planners had been convinced that new housing could only be built from Three Bridges south to Pease Pottage. Ministry rules finally allowed one car space or garage to every home.

St Richard's, *c.* 1953. The first Anglican church between St John's in the High Street and Worth's Saxon church, it served a community that had 6,511 residents in nearly 2,000 homes by 1966.

St Richard's, Three Bridges. Consecrated in July 1954, it was much admired by Housing Minister Harold Macmillan; when Prime Minister he was observed showing friends round it one Sunday.

A Sunday school class at Langley Green community hut, *c*. 1956. Wooden huts near each parade were used for dances, sales, socials, and meetings. New Towners were knitted together through such activities. The huts reserved land for better community centres.

Elizabeth Harland, celebrating her sixtieth birthday, October 1974. Seen with Miss Wragg and Miss Edwards at the Housing Office, she was known to thousands of tenants.

Langley Green's bus service started in May 1954. From March it had been a ghost service, with crews and vehicles allocated but the route unfinished. The first bus of the day was too late for factory workers but the last was timed around the cinema closing.

Gales Drive, Three Bridges, September 1953. Work on some nearby homes stopped at the first floor until the overhead power cables were taken down and buried. From here to the High Street was a sea of mud; A.P.V. workers crossed fields to the Northgate café where coaches collected them for Wandsworth.

Oak Way, Northgate, showing the old hedge line in the trees. Bungalows (far centre) were built in most neighbourhoods as the Corporation sought a mixed-age population. Hundreds of New Town settlers applied to bring their parents to Crawley.

Building Hazelwick Avenue, *c.* 1960. This view looks north with Hazelwick School's playing fields far right. The waterlogged ground almost swallowed a tracked construction vehicle. It was pulled free after thirty minutes.

Digging out a digger. The new main road from Three Bridges station to Manor Royal was between The Birches and the river. The sinking digger was watched and filmed by Brian Champion, who was late for work in Croydon that morning.

Crawley bus station, 1960. This was sited between the new railway station and the shopping centre.

Reeves and Huntley at Three Bridges had been a garage but developed a coal delivery business. The new Haslett Avenue ended through traffic.

Ethel 'Jane' Fraser cooked for construction workers who got her to pose as a surveyor. She moved from Alperton to Northgate to look after her grandchildren.

Administration buildings, The Boulevard, c. 1963. Jane Fraser worked on the Woodall Duckham site beyond the Town Hall.

Northgate School. Temporary classrooms had gone by 1956. 'Nearly every Northgate home had kids,' said a Paddington man recalling Crawley in the 1950s.

Fire station, opened 1957. Volunteer firemen were summoned by siren until the New Town's size justified a professional fire service. The continuing inaction over a new hospital, outside the Corporation's control, saw a Ministry of Health enquiry in 1958.

SECTION THREE

Employment

The Manor Royal industrial estate was inconveniently distant from the centre's shops, and factories had staff transport for midday shopping to keep their female workers. The mass of bicycles seen in the 1950s reduced as living standards changed, but cars and buses congested the few roads instead.

Staff changed jobs (draughtsmen were very nomadic) and some commuted to London. When Redifon needed to house thirty new staff in 1960, ministry file HLG 91/767 reveals that the Corporation had supplied 746 homes for their workers but it then employed only 642 people. In January 1961 The People said that housing restrictions were crippling Crawley and that the government 'won't let the Boom Town Boom!' In mid-1965 there were twenty jobs for every unemployed person in Crawley. The airport employed 1,200 in 1958 when it was reopened; in 1967 it employed 5,200.

Sometimes work was short: Silentbloc had women on a four-day week in 1956, and 250 at Paramount worked four days too. Strikes included 150 out at Redifon in August 1955, 800 at A.P.V. in April 1956 for three weeks, and a shut-down at Edwards which lasted nearly six months in 1962. The Edwards strike is thought to have involved powerful interests in a 'who runs British industry?' struggle.

By the mid-1960s the original 50,000 population plan was abandoned. In 1966 the population was 63,800 and it was estimated there would be 81,480 inhabitants by 1971.

Industrial estate, from the west, *c.* 1950. One couple had a picnic on this grass at the London Road end of Manor Royal. This view was seen by travellers, and the Corporation erected a sign advising those who wanted homes in Crawley to contact Miss Wragg.

The first large employer. Charlie Youngman brought his wooden ladder firm from Battersea and 'Leda' chrome bathroom fittings from Vauxhall, employing nearly 300 by 1954. West Green was named Youngman's Green by humorists.

Standard Factories. The first factories were ready in late 1950. Vaughan Lift, Bale & Church, A.S. Ladley and Test House Equipment were the first four New Town companies. They had 170 employees by 1954.

Youngman's ladder business boomed when timber from Canada and Scandinavia ceased to be rationed. It is said that Charlie Youngman purchased good timber at low prices in 1953 by clearing London's streets of the Coronation viewing stands.

Standard Factories, Crompton Way. Large firms had factories designed round their needs, but Vaughan Lift was happy to move here in October 1950. Its dozen staff had relocated by March 1951.

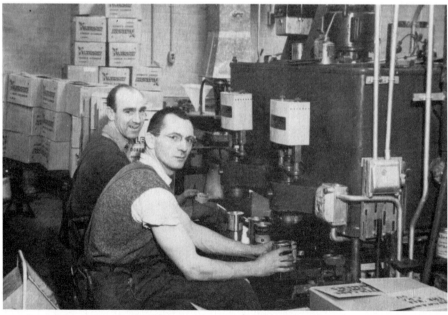

'Kleenoff' oven cleaner was made by Bale & Church in Crompton Way. The employees included John Larner (left) and Tony Leader. Their St Mary-at-Hall, Billingsgate operation was cramped, on the third floor, and deliveries of caustic soda were hoisted by an outside crane.

A.E. Bale founded Bale & Church. Nephew Richard Bale (right) ran the business. Ernie Wrench (standing) and Beryl Newman were among the seven staff out of thirteen who relocated. They paid 2s 7d, then 3s 1d workman's return fare until the company moved in late 1950.

Employees' families visiting the new workplace, 1950. Wives and children visited the New Town's industrial estate. This was the Standard Factory in Crompton Way for Vaughan Lift.

A.P.V.'s factory, 1951. This was built by James Longley's construction company, which had been in Crawley since 1881. When a craftsman living in Hove transferred to Longley's the Corporation would house his family only after the vacancy was advertised in London.

A.P.V.'s main building, 1951. From 1952 personnel were rehoused with their jobs following within months. Some wives discovered from reports in a local newspaper that their husbands had a substantial bonus every six months. Crawley shops were thought to raise prices in the week A.P.V. paid that bonus.

A.P.V.'s factory in farmland, *c*. 1954. Workers who moved to the New Town got a coach to Wandsworth, sometimes pushing it up Reigate Hill. A.P.V. and the Corporation arranged that work sections and staff moved within weeks of each other.

A.P.V., Manor Royal. A.P.V. buzzed with workers interested in sports, dancing, fishing, drama, and gardening (the company arranged bulk buying of seeds etc). A barber called two mornings a week.

A.P.V.'s stylish entrance stairs were an example of advanced engineering in 1951. The prototype Paraflow beneath it, later donated to the Science Museum, was a high temperature, short-time milk pasteurization machine invented in 1923. Paraflows were supplied to dairies, but it was years before the British government legislated for milk pasteurization, despite the knowledge that bovine tuberculosis harmed people and could kill.

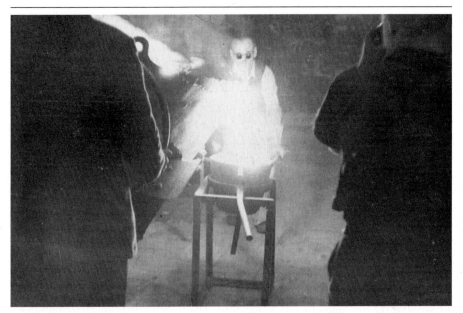

A.P.V. Paramount's foundry. Up to five hundred people worked for A.P.V. Paramount. Molten steel weighing 157 lb was carried by two men who ran to pour it into moulds. There was a foundry at Supatap makers F.H. Bourner which relocated from Croydon between 1951 and 1952.

One ton of steel was produced in one hour at Paramount's quickest furnace, with seven tons in production at one time. It was very hot but well-paid work. Twelve-hour shifts were normal. There was a waiting list of men anxious to work at Paramount.

Making a milk homogenizer base at A.P.V. Milk and beer processing outlets grew to include wine, ice cream and yoghurt, in Britain and all over the world.

Les James at A.P.V, making equipment for the nuclear industry.

The staff of Crawley Industrial Products, January 1950. This company was part of Frank Ayling's group, made up of Crawley Crates, Crawley Tools, Crawley Industrial Products, H. & E. Lintott of Horsham, Holmbush Potteries and Offen Precision Tools of South Nutfield. Crawley Tools started in 1938, Crawley Crates in 1945; this meant that like Jack Bowthorpe's companies they were not included in the Development Corporation's allocation of homes. This stand was erected for Princess Elizabeth's visit.

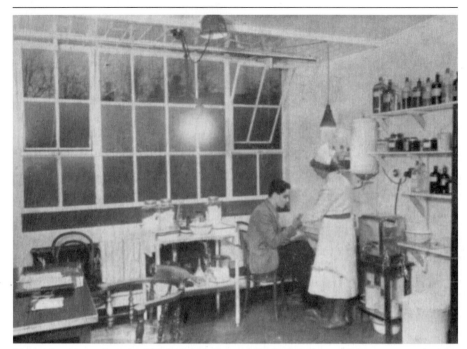

First aid room at Crawley Tools, 1951. Free medical advice to staff began around 1949, with Nurse Wood (above) in charge. Local GP Dr J.R.M. Vance was employed. These facilities were as good as Crawley's Cottage Hospital.

Travelling showroom for Crawley Crates, 1951. Few people had cars in 1951, so the planned motorway (later M23) was futuristic. Employees were not allowed to park on Manor Royal's roads, but government penny pinching forced the Corporation to ignore the need for garages and parking for twenty years.

Youngman imported Italian equipment. Working at this assembly belt machine are, left to right: Ivy Charman, -?-, Elsie Perkins, -?-, Daphne ?, and Vera Knott, a mix of New and Old Towners.

Two-ton crane for New Zealand, made in Crompton Way by Vaughan Lift. Several times bombed out, and housed in a leaking building in Featherstone Street near Old Street, Jason Vaughan's company had the Industrial Development Certificate that was required to get into the New Town.

Crompton Way in the 1950s, looking towards the London Road. Problems facing London manufacturers of bulky goods in the 1950s were reduced by relocating, but delivering to the customer was still a problem.

Fields Garage, High Street, late 1950s. Victor Wakefield works on a Beetle. John Leppard ran Fields, which had been on the east side of the High Street behind the trees. His wife Margaret was a teacher. Their staff parties were well-mixed and enjoyable.

Vitamins Ltd site ceremony, June 1952. A cramped Thames-side factory in Hammersmith was quite different to Magpie Wood. The woman in the trench (left) is Dr Wright. To her left is factory manager D.W. Bicheno, then Gordon Flint and Miss Ellis. Director Mr Groves is nearest the camera, with Bemax production manager May Newell on his right.

J.H. Wrentmore of Vitamins Ltd. The 88 year old senior director adds his weight at the site ceremony on 7 June 1952. In 1955 2,500,000 pills were produced at the factory. The company magazine *The Germ* kept employees aware of Crawley and the relocation, which was completed by August 1956.

Jack Bowthorpe, February 1952. Moved away from wartime Croydon aerodrome to Oxford, Bowthorpe (second left) relocated to Tinsley Lane in 1948. W. Puckey (centre) of the aircraft production section of the Ministry of Supply opened the factory four years later.

Workers Playtime radio show, *c.* 1960. Nearly six hundred were in the canteen at Bowthorpe to enjoy the 30 minute BBC radio programme. Bert Weedon (guitar) is on comedian Cardew Robinson's right, and singer David Hughes is on Robinson's left.

Bowthorpe's internationalism, *c.* 1960. Bowthorpe's *Contact* magazine noted that Crawley 'has a somewhat cosmopolitan flavour about it'. Back, left to right: Mrs Lebber (Finland), Mr Barbans (Latvia), Mr L. Lazazzara (Italy), G. Benilla (Gibraltar), A. Raichura (Uganda), Bob Rokach (Austria), Mrs Petryszyn (Italy). Front: Mrs Skibinska and Mrs J. Luczka (Poland), Mrs H. Rokach (Austria), Mrs D. Gray (Germany), Mrs T. Cerabono and Mrs Urvivioli (Italy), Mrs Mielnik (Poland), Mrs M. Venes (Austria).

The sweet factory. A.H. Scrase's Young, Randall & Co. Ltd moved in 1952 to make Sun d'Or sweets and chocolates in modern, larger premises compared with those at Lansdowne Road, East Croydon. Forty key staff moved to Crawley. Sun d'Or had 150 mainly female workers. Hours were adjusted so they could get their families' evening meals by starting at 7.30 a.m., taking 30 minutes lunch break, and stopping at 4 p.m.

The staff of Edwards at Lower Sydenham, 1953. Up to seventeen coaches took employees from Crawley to south-east London until the firm relocated. Companies including Stone and A.P.V. had coaches for months. Others paid railway fares. Motor cars were reaching working people, but the New Town's road widths were restricted by the ministry, as were garages. The Corporation put several road-access allotments on the plans for Tilgate. They became car parks as anticipated.

Frederick Edwards, *c.* 1954. Cramped factory premises were eased by spreading into space in a college at Lower Sydenham but Edwards had looked at the Southern Aircraft Co.'s site in Tinsley Lane in 1945 and at Salfords in Surrey before deciding on Crawley. From 1951, 250 to 300 staff were rehoused. Edwards' factory was officially opened in March 1954.

Another Edwards coach.

Long-service staff at Edwards, *c.* 1975. These employees had joined before Edwards moved from Lower Sydenham. Standing, left to right: Eric Ryder, Joe Osborne, -?-, -?-, Ben Williams, -?-, Terry Rowe, Bill Rouse, Nigel Dennis(?), -?-, Tony Syrett. Seated: Ken Coe with three forgotten veterans, Stan Large, Ron Frei behind Bill Smith, -?-, -?-, -?-, -?-.

LCON WATER STORAGE TOWER

The Telegraph Construction and Maintenance Co. Ltd started production in Crawley in late 1954. Like others, it had taken months to completely relocate (from Greenwich). Nearly three hundred worked for Telcon.

Renate Warner and a Brentford's transformer. Fellow German refugee Martin Rosenfeld established his transformer factory in Brentford in 1935. In 1956 she arranged Brentford Transformers Ltd's staff relocation to Crawley from Kidbrooke. Over half of the 270 relocated.

South Eastern Electricity Board social, *c.* 1951. St Peter's, West Green, had a hall that was used by Old and New Towners. The Congregational church hall in Robinson Road was larger.

Lloyd's Register of Shipping of Southwark Street near London Bridge was bomb damaged and cramped. Unable to expand, chairman Sir Ronald Garrett had the idea of relocating after meeting one of the New Town chairmen. In 1950 or 1951 the staff with wives visited Crawley, dining at Broadfield as guests of the Development Corporation, and the next time, less grandly, in The Sun public house. Crawley, being ahead of other New Towns, was chosen for the new site. At the beginning of 1953 the printing machinery was moved to Manor Royal. As the print trade was centred in London half of the staff refused to move. New people, prepared to relocate, were employed and trained. Homes were available in a choice of styles and neighbourhoods. Access to Three Bridges station was desired as many realized that the New Town had no other employment for printers. Once moved, by late 1953, some found night shift work in London and commuted. That skilled workers had refused to move is not shown in the annual reports. The planners assumed that relocated workers would stay with their employer or move back to London. Commuting was possible, and may have been encouraged during the months that staff travelled to Manor Royal from their London homes. Lloyd's produced an annual list of ships in two large volumes, as well as rules for testing and classifying ships. Quarterly reports of ships under construction, wrecks and losses, and new names, were printed in Crawley, which had 'more breathing space'.

Felco Hoists of Crawley purchased Jason Vaughan's lift and pulley company, which had forty-seven workers by 1954.

Felco Hoists on Gatwick Road near Napier Way. The round extractor fan in the window was manufactured by Vent-Axia, which moved from Putney to Fleming Way in April 1959.

Axia Fans and Vent-Axia, Fleming Way, *c.* 1959. Cramped at Palfrey Place near The Oval, with a corner shop converted into a store, and transporting fans to Vent-Axia in Putney for testing, Axia Fans relocated in August 1958. Shop-floor workers were collected in Brixton for six months until they relocated or committed themselves to London. Several moved to Tilgate which a pioneer settler remembered had 'nobody there' and was 'desolate' in 1958. In April 1959 Vent-Axia, another Joe Akester company, moved here. Women predominated on its assembly lines. The spectacular sunsets, visible from the draughtsmen's office on the first floor, and a dozen cows which got in to the factory, were reminders that Crawley was in the country. A spate of payroll robberies saw a police helicopter land nearby. The estate's growth led to major factories agreeing to stagger their hours to avoid a five o'clock traffic jam.

Marine and factory extractor fans, *c*. 1964. J. and E. Hall of Dartford was the major customer for marine fans made in Crawley by Axia Fans. Hall's bought the company, selling it in 1968 when this factory closed.

Vent-Axia, 1971. Axia Fans was sold off and the factory taken on by KDG after Vent-Axia moved across Newton Road to this site.

Priestly Way, *c.* 1967. Fourteen workshops were built for local firms, often set up by ambitious ex-employees who subcontracted for New Town firms.

SECTION FOUR

Rent Strike

Crawley New Town rents were high. Parliament noted this in 1952, and Dr Clout told fellow parish councillors the same in mid-1953. The LCC charged much less, although its three-bedroom homes were difficult to get.

Lord Wilmot, previously Labour MP John Wilmot, chaired Edwards in 1953 when he told the government that disquiet over high rents could be exploited by Communists 'seeking to ferment industrial unrest'. In 1955 Conservative MP and war hero Freddie Gough said that the Crawley Tenants' Association 'has an extremely left-wing bias', as it held meetings and organized the rent strike.

Early settlers believed that as sitting tenants their rents were fixed. Yet building costs and land prices rose with every neighbourhood and the Corporation decided that all New Town homes should pay the same, rejecting different payment levels in different neighbourhoods which the minister suggested in April 1953.

Some who marched paid the new rent; others paid just the old, and some paid nothing. Bennett reported that 56 per cent paid higher rent immediately, and 21 per cent after one month. Everyone was paying by mid-February 1956. However, one fifth of New Towners, or 1,100 homes, continued the protest more than one month after the march.

CRAWLEY TENANTS' ASSOCIATION

newsletter

SEPTEMBER, 1953   No. 4   PRICE 2d.

THIS ISSUE OF THE NEWSLETTER IS ENTIRELY DEVOTED TO THE REPORT OF THE RENTS COMMITTEE. COME ALONG AND GIVE US YOUR VIEWS ON IT AT THE GENERAL MEMBERS MEETING ON SEPTEMBER 2th IN THE CONGREGATIONAL HALL AT 8 p.m.

Focus on Rents . . .

The Central Executive Committee have no hesitation in recommending all members to give their full support to the following report. The burden of high rents is generally acknowledged to be a heavy one. At the present level, and especially in the face of rising living costs, it is impossible for even the best-paid tenants to maintain a decent standard of living, let alone provide themselves with any reserve against illness, short-time or unemployment.

We want to see the original plans for the New Town carried out in full. But this will be impossible if so little is left out of the family income, after the rent is paid. For it means that less will be spent in the shops and on entertainments, so that their development will be held back. So in turn will be the growth of rateable value, causing Local Authority services also to lag behind the growth of population.

The object of this Report is to show ways in which reductions in rents can be achieved, thus avoiding further hardship and helping to balance the economy of the New Town.

In concluding this introduction, we wish to place on record our sincere appreciation of all the very hard work which has been put into the compilation of the Report by the Rents Committee.

For the Central Executive Committee:
VIC PELLEN (*Chairman*)
HAZEL LeMAGE (*Secretary*)
TONY STOKER (*Asst. Secretary*)
7th September, 1953

REPORT

OF THE

RENTS COMMITTEE

The Rents Committee was set up on the instructions of a General Members' Meeting of the Association on 27th November, 1952.

Its terms of reference were:

" to investigate the reasons for the high rents locally, and, having determined the causes, to take vigorous action for their abatement."

The Rents Committee was to be composed of representatives of the C.T.A., together with delegates from local Trade Union organisations, and all political parties in the town who would agree to co-operate.

The following organisations have been represented on the Rents Committee:

C.T.A.   Central Executive Committee
Northgate Neighbourhood
Three Bridges Neighbourhood
West Green Neighbourhood
Crawley Trades Council
Amalgamated Engineering Union, Crawley
Amalgamated Society of Woodworkers, Crawley
Amalgamated Union of Building Trade Workers, Crawley
Transport and General Workers' Union (Composite Branch)
Transport and General Workers' Union (Transport Branch)
A.P.V. Shop Stewards' Committee
Crawley Co-operative Women's Guild
Crawley Communist Party
Crawley Labour Party

Crawley rents were high. In May 1952 the ministry noted that Crawley charged 50 per cent more than the LCC.

Rent protestors at Manor Royal, October 1955. Mike Syrett photographed marchers setting off behind a band to the town centre. It had been arranged that as the band passed, workers would down tools and join on.

Rent protest at the Broadwalk. Crawley Tenants' Association headed five thousand marchers including women with prams. Asked about eviction for non-payment an A.P.V. employee growled 'They'll lose the whole of A.P.V. first'.

'Not a Penny on the Rent.' Mike Syrett captured the concern over the first rent increase. A two-bedroom house was now 30s and a five-bedroom house nearly two pounds a week. Few had paid so much before they were rehoused.

Crouch bricklayers dispute, *c*. 1953. G.T. Crouch had four disputes at Langley Green in 1953. 'If you ask for more money you are branded a Communist' noted the *Courier* in January 1954.

SECTION FIVE

Shopping

Living in Sussex did not mean country food, as one pioneer discovered when informed that his greengrocer purchased at the Borough Market in Southwark. Early settlers in Langley Green discovered that a nearby turkey farm and fifty pigs were very smelly.

Small-town habits continued as the population trebled, with midday closing on Saturdays lasting into 1954. Greenyer's self-service shop in the Broadwalk opened until 8 p.m. on Fridays from October 1955. Shops delivered but did not welcome hire purchase. Major items of furniture were often purchased in old haunts in London, and Londoners missed a street market.

Traders called with cockles, muffins and crumpets, fresh fish from Hastings, insurance policies, brushes and Provident cheques. The canteen manager at Edwards sold meat until he was told to stop. The Corporation took bids for shops on the parades, and found newsagents bid double the greengrocer or fish shop. The mix of shops was fixed by the Corporation, which inspected shops run by would-be tenants.

Working on the Broadwalk, November 1953. A couple, thought to be in their nineties, was rehoused in Smalls Mead at the same tiny rent they had paid for a damp cottage here.

The Broadwalk, c. 1956. The Corporation allowed Old Town shops to relocate for the same rent, but most leases were taken up by multiples or by traders new to the town.

Crawley's shopping centre, February 1954. Gas had been piped 20 miles from Croydon; 25 miles of road had been built; the plan for Southgate was complete and that for Tilgate had started; and the Corporation expected to have completed 4,000 homes by 1955.

Queens Square in the mid-1950s. Getting from Three Bridges neighbourhood to the High Street took one through building sites as the central shopping area spread east.

Queens Square had traffic on the northern side, and a fountain designed by J. Bainbridge Copnall. By March 1957, 50 of 122 shops in the new centre were trading.

The Broadwalk at the High Street, opened in December 1954. Teenagers gathered here on Saturday afternoons, attracted by the pop records played in the electrical shop near the Brewery Shades.

West Green parade, *c.* 1954. Ewhurst Road beyond had some of the fifty-five detached houses with garages built by the Corporation for rent or sale (at £3,000–£3,800) between 1953 and 1954. They generally housed company directors.

Langley Green parade. The fish and chip shop, run by the Kingston family, had queues every Friday and Saturday evening.

Northgate shops, *c*. 1955. The pharmacy, not the post office, had the pillar box. A mistake not widely known was that the flats above all had the same front door key.

The shoe repairer at Northgate. One family from Clapham was pleased to discover that Jackson, the shoe repairer at Ifield around 1960, was from their part of London.

The market had fourteen stalls in 1955. Hedley V. Wilkinson of Wag's Stores was the cheapest shop until Tesco came to Crawley.

Gales Drive shops, Three Bridges. The early settlers shopped in North Road, the old Three Bridges High Street, the Co-op in Hazelwick Road and at Eastwood nursery before this parade was ready. Mr Emerson (centre), the tobacconist, was blind.

Ifield parade shops, *c*. 1958. Mothers found the town centre too far to go with children. Pathways were poor. One early settler spoke to nobody and went without fresh vegetables for three months while her husband worked the overtime they needed to pay for furniture.

The Pelham Buckle, Ifield opened in December 1957. Legislation that New Town pubs should sell beer from the State-owned brewery in Carlisle had been repealed in 1952.

Pound Hill shops, *c. 1957*. Butcher Ron Portlake created a stir by supplying cheap meat to pensioners and, in mid-1956, selling cut-price vegetables from a farm.

Tilgate Parade, *c. 1960*. Cinders were walked into shops until paving stones were laid. A 1957 settler recalled buying eggs and vegetables from a smallholding at the dam at Tilgate lake.

Southgate's Wakehurst Drive parade was welcomed, for this neighbourhood was distant from the town centre. Southgate homes lacked central heating which, in 1957, was being fitted in new London homes.

Queens Square, c. 1962. Placing the Gatwick racecourse bandstand in the square helped, but the New Town's centre was dull, although at least it had no high-rise blocks. Note the bicycles.

The curved Tilgate Parade so impressed official visitors from Yugoslavia that they took this photograph. Its design suggests that the barrack-like Queens Square did not have to be so dull.

Queens Square, *c.* 1959. Shops opened in time for Christmas 1957, and gave employment to many women. Woolworth relocated from the Grand Parade and nearly doubled its staff to seventy.

Gossops Green (once called Gossip's Green), *c.* 1964. Settlers from 1959 had the same problems as other neighbourhoods: no pavements and no shops, apart from a mobile Co-op twice a week. It was difficult to get to the High Street. Getting to Thomas Bennett School involved a change of bus.

Furnace Green parade, 1968. Several iron workings in this valley revealed during construction led the neighbourhood to be named after Furnace Farm, and not Tilgate East. Later neighbourhoods were located outside the ring road or east of the railway.

Fields Garage, High Street, *c.* 1970. When the High Street was the road between London and Brighton, selling petrol and servicing vehicles was good business.

Tesco in the High Street. Even Wag's Stores in the market could not match Tesco prices. Bicycles are absent: the mini car and double yellow lines had triumphed.

The Fox at Three Bridges station, August 1964. A few years earlier the flooded river reached to the first floor and no vehicle passed under the railway bridge.

Crawley New Town centre, c. 1978. The old Three Bridges Road (lower right) passes the parish church and Memorial Gardens. The George Hotel extension (bottom) and Sussex House (next to the cinema, lower left) were new aspects of the High Street.

The Clock, Queens Square. A complicated but delightful show of old-style cars, in honour of the annual Old Crocks Race, was part of the clock, but malfunctioned so often it was removed.

Queensway Stores. National chain-store groups opened branches in Crawley as the New Town's population kept growing. In 1955/6 six thousand people moved to Crawley.

Motor cars for shopping. The central streets were designed without awareness of the spread of car ownership. Other new towns segregated pedestrians and vehicles, forcing people to use subways.

Old trees on The Boulevard. One of the earliest maps drawn by the Development Corporation showed mature trees and hedgerows. Architects and builders had to design round them, and their roots, which increased building costs.

The Queens Square fountain. Cars could park in the square.

Crawley's coach station. Young people took a Southdown coach to dances at the Handcross village hall.

Old Three Bridges Road at the High Street with Station Road (with its police station) at the rear. The level crossing still caused delays, for plans to have a road over it were rejected by the government.

SECTION SIX

Carnival

Held on a Whitsun Monday, the carnival parade lined up near Hermits Road in Three Bridges. The industrial companies drove their grand floats from the nearby estate. Secret plans and considerable efforts went into the floats. Bowthorpe won in 1954, and two or three years later with their 'Trial of the Knave of Hearts'. In 1958 Longley won. Three years later the winner had young ladies dancing round a maypole in Old and New Sussex.

Social and sports clubs, groups and associations put in entries. In 1959 the Central Band of the Royal Air Force was not amused to be outstaged by a group of New Orleans-style jazz men who gatecrashed the parade.

The carnival committee was chaired by Jack Bowthorpe, whose cashier Johnny Dymock was a stalwart. In 1968 its organization was passed to the Lions.

When business boomed the factories allowed staff to spend hours preparing the floats; in recessions, although time was available, the interest diminished. Participation was fun: thousands lined the streets. The manned signal-box at the level crossing held back the trains at carnival time.

Crawley Crates carnival entry, 1951. Driver Arthur Revell towed around a dozen colleagues. This was the prize-winner.

'Inspection and Welfare 1851–1951' was the theme of Crawley Crates entry, which was later entered for Horsham's carnival.

Early 1950s carnival queen. It all seems very serious.

UNITED EFFORT MEANS SUCCE[SS]

HELP YOUR HOSPITAL

Hospital appeal at the carnival. The man with the spade is Vic Pellen, so is this the Tenants' Association float?

The carnival, May 1951, outside the George Hotel.

The carnival in the early 1950s. A cup of tea at the Northgate café was often a New Towner's first experience of Crawley. Cyclists had used its accommodation, which was full of labourers now.

Crawley Motor Cycle Club in the carnival, *c.* 1953. Prizes were awarded in several categories, from the largest firms to clubs.

Bowthorpe-Hellermann's 1957 float was King Henry VII and his court. Hellermann had supplied Bowthorpe until the war, and sold out to Jack Bowthorpe in 1957. Bowthorpe's expansion led to a factory at East Grinstead, due to labour shortages in Crawley.

The 'Trial of the Knave of Hearts', *c. 1956*. Bowthorpe won the Best Decorated Vehicle (Industrial) award in the carnival with this. The knave was Alf Jones, Alice was Jenny Whyte, the card soldiers were John Miles and John Cole, Heather Hollands was the Queen, the white rabbit was Robert Foster, and Betty Miles was the dormouse.

Approaching the level crossing, Bowthorpe's float has Charles Flynn as a fish footman driving the tractor. The firm's maintenance department built this to an idea developed by Reg Conlon and Ernie Cost.

Carnival queen, May 1958. Left to right: Shirley Scheepers from South Africa, radio personality Jack Train, Maureen Rowe, 'problems page' writer Edana Romney, and Valerie Worth. The contest was reported in the London *Evening Standard*.

The carnival parade in front of the college. Large firms spent hours working on their floats, using expert staff including exhibition stand designers, painters, and carpenters. The judges took that professionalism into account.

The carnival queen, *c.* 1952.

Young sailors at the carnival, *c.* 1965. Did these youngsters actually ride on this overloaded vehicle?

Jazzing the parade, 1959. Crawley's New City Jazzmen with friends from Burgess Hill, London, and Brighton, formed a parade band and gatecrashed the carnival. The Central Band of the RAF was the official band but the jazzers were cheered.

The Excelsior jazz band of 1959 included this sousaphone player.

Carnival beauties, *c.* 1960. The Whitsun holiday carnival was a non-political public exhibition of the New Town by the people of Crawley.

The carnival, 1964. Building and Civil Engineering Holidays Scheme was a white-collar employer. Office jobs for school leavers were normal by the 1960s. If relatives could put in a good word it helped, and some firms had many related employees.

SECTION SEVEN

Leisure

The Tenants' Association organized dances and outings but grew more political. The Community Association's committee had representatives from many areas of New Town life. The simple yet effective community huts knitted together the migrants. Five were open by 1956. They were centres for neighbourhoods of strangers.

Northgate's junior rock 'n' roll club had been 'short-lived – rather to the relief of the Secretary' noted the November 1956 Community Association's report. Dancing classes, union meetings, jumble sales and wedding receptions were held in the huts. Club meetings were held in them and in schools.

Cyclists had two clubs. The Crawley and District Choir was founded in 1958 and soon had thirty-six members. An angling society was founded in 1957. Scout and guide groups were formed as each neighbourhood was occupied; the 4th Worth and 1st Crawley Scouts were long established. In 1957 an Operatic Society was formed. From parents and teachers at Thomas Bennett School a choral group emerged. The Lions started in 1962. Amateur dramatics were found in a Tilgate Forest Army hut and, from 1973, at the Ifield Barn. Pubs, darts teams, sea fishing, gardening, and voluntary groups from the Red Cross to Sunday schools, all kept people busy.

The Peter Frazer Band, *c.* 1960. Pianist Albert Frackleton was from Cork; Pete Fry (drums), Reg Fisher (bass) and Morris Harding (guitar) were from London. They played for dinner dances and at all the community huts, with Latin American rhythms very popular.

Brett Marvin and the Thunderbolts, formed in 1968. As Terrydactyl and the Dinosaurs their *Seaside Shuffle* was in the Top Ten in 1972, which led to television work. The founders were Graham Hine, Keith Tussell, John Randall, Pete Gibson and Jim Pitts. Randall is second left, with Gibson on his left.

Champions of British Barber-shop, 1961. John Danser (left), David Steele (next to him) and Bob Witherington (right) formed a barber-shop quartet in 1960. John and Tony Danser (second from right) went to the USA in 1964. Crawley's quartet was national champion four times.

The Crawley Barber-shop Harmony Club, November 1964. Back, left to right: -?-, John Noyce, -?-, Tom Rostron, Bob Witherington. Middle: John Danser, Harold Barnhurst, George Howe, Ernest Short, Dennis Cullip and Harry Danser. Front: Bob Doddington, Tony Danser.

The Grasshopper pub, Tilgate. Manager John Bennett hired groups and comedians, and put on talent nights. Its hall was hired for dances. Renting a whole house instead of a few rooms left few New Towners with much spare cash, and there were the temptations of the 'never-never' or hire purchase for furniture and cookers. By the time Tilgate was completed, the 1960s boom saw the factories and airport paying good money, with overtime on offer too. Many homes had televisions, and old socializing patterns changed.

Radio 'Goon' Harry Secombe at a celebrity cricket match at Jordans. At an earlier A.P.V. cricket match at Three Bridges Secombe confessed that he had believed it was the television giant A.T.V. which had invited him. Secombe's television career came later.

Traditional jazz jivers in Queens Square, 1958. There were weekend dances above Leon's fashion shop, and at the Starlight Ballroom. Handcross village hall and halls in Purley and Brighton were also dance venues.

The jazz singer, 1958. Brenda Morgan with the New City Jazzmen. Formed at the El Salvador coffee bar between the Railway Hotel and East Park, after informal sessions in the canteen of Crawley Metal Productions, this traditional jazz band played at Crawley Town's club house.

An evening at Jordans in the 1950s.

Agatha Christie's *Dry Rot* was presented at A.P.V., *c*. 1961. Catherine Ball is centre, with Peter Fold on the right.

Concordia sing Berlioz in a railway station, May 1972. Thomas Bennett School music teacher Ron Sampson founded and conducted Concordia from 1958. When the *Brighton Belle* was taken out of service, his choir sang the 'Railway Song' with military bands on the platform.

Carl Orff's 'Carmina Burana' at St Wilfrid's School, *c.* 1972. Between seventy and a hundred choristers were members of Concordia.

Crawley Operatic Society's 'Summer Song', 1971. At St Wilfrid's School are, left to right: Gwyn Roberts, Margaret Withers, Beryl Oatey, Louis Maule-Cole, Barbara Gittins, Ted Hartwell, Jack Allen, Robert Wise.

'Summer Song' performers in 1971 included bass Ken Stephens (centre) who was from Trinidad. Louis Maule-Cole played Dvorak (with beard, to right).

Crawley bus depot's darts team and friends, *c.* 1958. Back, left to right: Gordon Nightingale, -?-, Jack Perkins, George Christensen behind Bert Walpole, Paddy ? (later a pub landlord), Ricky Rickson, -?-, Jack Packham, -?-, -?-. Front: Ron Spraggs, -?-, Herbert ?, Charlie Edwards, Arthur Nickson in front, -?-, Wilfred James, -?-.

A.P.V.'s annual dinner and dance, November 1956, at the Metropole Hotel in Brighton, was five years after the foundation stone had been laid at Manor Royal. The relocation had been completed in December 1955.

Crawley's first Chinese restaurant, the Marco Polo, opened at 38 The Broadway in 1960. The Chinese cook bought ingredients in London. 'It was ahead of its time' recalled the owner, London-born Mario Dezzani.

Mario Dezzani, *c.* 1961. His Café Mario opened in The Broadway in December 1957. 'Mr Mario' introduced frothy coffee and spaghetti to many. Open all week until the cinema emptied, it was popular with the young who listened to the juke box. 'The boys and girls wore the latest fashions,' said Mr Dezzani.

Milkmen, *c*. 1958. Jones of Ifield, Law's, Tom Gardner of the High Street, and Frank Reynolds' dairies merged over the years. Reynolds had temporary shops before the parades were built, and two shops in old West Green. Staff were recruited in London as milk sales boomed with so many children and residents arriving.

British Manufactured Bearings, new year party, *c*. 1952. The office was in Crawley and there were factories in Charlwood and behind The George. BMB had to bus workers to Charlwood, so the company relocated to Crawley's industrial estate, and later to Scotland.

The bishop and the ladies, *c.* 1953. Revd Geoffrey Warde, Bishop of Lewes, met representatives of the Mothers Union, the Young Wives of Crawley, and Three Bridges Young Wives Group.

Langley Green Young Wives Group, *c.* 1958. This was a 'tramps party' in the community hut. Some people joined in everything.

Three Bridges Young Wives Group.

Three Bridges Young Wives Group. There must have been a great deal of preparation to have such a formal meal in a hall.

Church dedication of the new ambulance, *c.* 1965. St John Ambulance Brigade's Divisional Officer Harry Farmer (front, left), with Ron Gilroy behind; Chris Smith and George Scott in line ahead of Dave Peachey, -?-, Jack Jarvis, with Roger Duke, Ted Reid and Darrel Birch behind them. Keith Wilson is obscured by the man on the pavement. John Freestone is ahead of Wilson. Hilda Wilson, Divisional Superintendent, leads the ladies, with Dorreen Strange on her right.

SECTION EIGHT

Sports and Games

There had been organized sports and games in the area for years, with cricket well established in Ifield and Three Bridges, soccer teams in Crawley and Three Bridges, and an athletics club. Local firms had teams. Some factories had sports fields nearby. A.P.V. purchased an old country club and added pitches and courts to make Jordans on the London Road a popular centre.

Many firms had a soccer team, sometimes several. New Towners added fresh muscle and spirit, and so helped expand existing clubs such as Three Bridges CC, which had been a wandering side until Worth Parish Council restored their old field in 1950. New blood enabled the rugby club to revive.

The nearest swimming pool was in Horsham unless you sneaked over the fence at Vitamins Ltd – an arrangement that was made formal after some time. Fishing was popular, with stories of A.P.V. men stopping with rod and line near Three Bridges station.

Crawley Athletic Club included founder Tom Lintern, with Jack Shelton and John Butler in enthusiastic support by 1959. Boxing was popular and the town had its own boxing club. Thomas Bennett would not have approved of the 1980s golf course.

Crawley Town FC, *c. 1953*. Standing, left to right: Sammy Hoad, Norris 'Bunny' Hall, Phil Bastable, Fred Stenning, Ken Cheesman, Doug Bastable, George Parker, (?) Ernie Dennett. Front: Tommy Ryan, Bernard Barker, Tom Jarvie, -?-, Wilf Cole. Jarvie, a veterinary surgeon, had been capped for Scotland before the war.

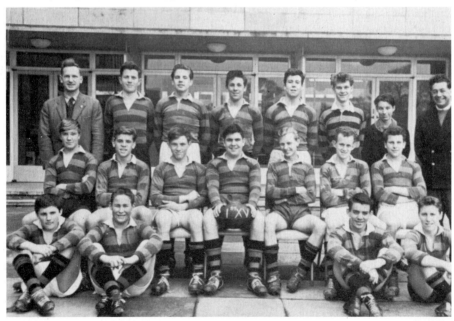

Sarah Robinson School, Ifield, 1950s. Few Londoners played rugby and David Polhill regretted that his pupils were keener on soccer.

Three Bridges Cricket Club Colts, *c.* 1972. Left to right: Dennis Brigden, Paul Parker (later capped for England), Howard Yardy, Nick Janik, John Gorringe, -?-, -?-, Linda Brigden, Steve Bennett, Julian Bennett, -?-, Mike Douglas, Dave Evans, Geoff Brown.

Three Bridges v. Sussex, *c.* 1958. Left to right: Francis Trist, Terry Evans, Reg Marshall, Les Kampster, Dick Austin, Ted Styles, Mike Harvey, Len Lenham and Jim Parks (two Sussex players), George Evans behind, Bernard Barker, Sussex benefit star Ted James, Ian Thompson (rear), Ted Dexter (the famed Sussex and England player), Richard Langridge, Terry Gunn (rear), Dan Smith, Peter Leddon, George Cox of Sussex (who had played for Arsenal), Bob Pountain.

Tony Barnes wins the 880 yards final in the Sussex Junior Championship, 1960. A member of the Crawley Athletic Club from 1959, he won the 1961 one mile and 1963 six miles Seniors, and was in the Crawley AC team that won the Sussex Junior cross-country championship. Behind him is Chris Carter of Hove AC.

Crawley Town Minors, c. 1951. Standing, left to right: Albert Welch (manager), Derek Lee, David Yaxley, John Pollard, Frank Verbeeten, Gerald Roberts, Roy Brackpool, Ernie Dennett (trainer). Seated: John Simmonds, Richard Green, Eric Tullet, Albert Green, Billy Ashton, Brian Bayliss. Welch and the Green brothers were New Towners.

Crawley rugger team, 8 March 1952. Clothes were rationed and two-colour shirts impossible to find. Back, left to right: R.B. Vernon, D. Heckstall-Smith, K. Scholey, E. Miles, John Jaffe, Ian Wilcockson, H.W. Pickstone, David Polhill, Michael Longley, J. Newton (referee). Front: R. Piper, J. Comfort, F. Humphries, David Lloyd-Thomas, W.S. 'Jock' Donald, R. Bird, Selby Davies. The club's revival from 1950 was helped by Corporation staff and other New Towners including A.P.V. engineer John Jaffe.

Crawley rugger team, 1972. Back, left to right: Henry Grainger, Jack Chapman, John Bennett, Ray Lloyd, Tubby Truscott, Peter Smiley and his father Len, John Healey, Peter Miller. Front: Chris Hammond, Alan Ryrie, Cass Wilson, Anthony Figgins-Brickwood (whose fiftieth birthday match this was), David Polhill, Laurie Hickey, John Hammond. About this time pig farmer Eldon Griffiths, future Conservative MP, played for Crawley.

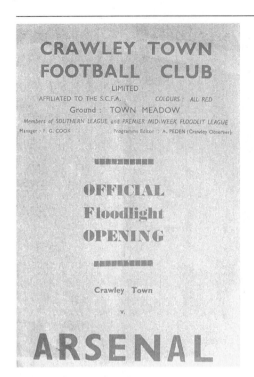

CRAWLEY TOWN FOOTBALL CLUB
LIMITED
AFFILIATED TO THE S.C.F.A. COLOURS : ALL RED
Ground : TOWN MEADOW
Members of SOUTHERN LEAGUE and PREMIER MID-WEEK FLOODLIT LEAGUE
Manager · F. G. COOK Programme Editor : A. PEDEN (Crawley Observer)

OFFICIAL Floodlight OPENING

Crawley Town
v.

ARSENAL

The London connection. Arsenal's visit to Crawley reminded many of the times they had attended London matches before moving to the New Town.

Crawley Town FC, 1963. Standing, left to right: D. Hollands, D. Waterman, C. Puddefat, D. Stripp, G. Jones, R. Finch, S. Marsh (trainer). Front: A. McCall, K. Parsons, R. Carter, B. Goldrick, A. Armstrong. The team was then playing in all-red.

A.P.V.'s angling club, 1956. Ron Twidale was the cup winner and Bill Billington (left) and Alf Avery won medals. Table tennis and lawn tennis, soccer, motor cycling, and athletics were some of the Athletic and Sports Club activities in 1956.

KDG's soccer team, c. 1964. Always playing away matches, this group of friends seldom won. Standing, left to right: John Gammon, Peter Stoneman, Bob Hurren, Reg Vince, Jim Brown, Ken Pratt, Doug Yeales. Front: Jack Hollington, Harry Lindsey, Fred Green, Dave Peacock, Jim Wilson (manager).

Crawley Young Athletes League, 1982. Taken at Withdean Stadium, Brighton. The 11 to 16 year olds were in the nation's top sixteen teams in 1984, and many were to be in the Senior Men's team which reached the United Kingdom finals.

SECTION NINE

Youngsters

The New Town had children everywhere. The migrants were young and ambitious, often living in the first place they could regard as their own home. The symbol of Crawley New Town could have been a washing-line of nappies.

The plan placed secondary schools – Hazelwick, Ifield, and Thomas Bennett – on the edge of neighbourhoods, grandly marking them 'campus'. They were not very convenient for night schools or for children in newer neighbourhoods. Thomas Bennett School was thought to be Europe's largest comprehensive school. It taught Russian, making some see Communists everywhere in the New Town.

Churches combined to teach children. Methodists, whose hall and church in Northgate were to be grand, shared Sunday school teaching with Anglicans. The Baptist minister encouraged children and parents to participate in activities. Two independent churches, solidly rooted in the pre-war community, welcomed New Towners.

National youth organizations were active. Dances were popular above Leon's dress shop, at the plush Starlight Ballroom and at the jazz club. The cinema and Mario's coffee bar attracted the young.

Crawley College, under the eagle eye of Dr Siklos, whose silent inspections terrified staff, trained apprentices and office workers for the New Town.

West Green Primary School children, *c.* 1953. Lessons were held in a hut. Ivy Stobbart (right) had moved to Crawley with evacuated London children in 1939.

Church of England Primary School, Ifield Road, *c.* 1954. During the war mornings were for Crawley children and afternoons for Londoners. Some evacuated children were adopted by Crawley couples. Catholics went to school near the friary.

Crawley Adventure Playground

Playground

"It takes courage, initiative and faith to organize an adventure playground, but I believe that few things today can be more rewarding".

LADY ALLEN OF HURTWOOD

PUBLISHED BY
**THE CRAWLEY COMMUNITY ASSOCIATION
ADVENTURE PLAYGROUND COMMITTEE**
CRAWLEY, SUSSEX   PRICE: TWO SHILLINGS

West Green had nine hundred schoolchildren. The supervisor welcomed timber from Youngman, sand from Percy Wales, barrels, nails, and breeze blocks. When timber ran low the children used sixty Army entrenching tools and made homes underground.

West Green adventure playground, 1954. The playground opened on 7 August from 1.30 p.m. to dusk or 8.00 p.m. Up to 150 children made houses, cooked potatoes, dug and played. It reopened all day in April 1955.

4th Worth Cubs at East Grinstead sports, 1952. Back, left to right: Michael Lee, Robert Stratton, Dick Manville (scoutmaster), Malcolm Wilson, Trevor Griffiths, DC Group Captain Pack. Middle: Tim Laker, Terry Luxford. Front: Robert Baker, Tony Mitchell, Michael Harvey, John Kirk, Richard Box.

Three Bridges scouting, Ifield 1954, with Alex Nash, the Group Leader of 1st Three Bridges (centre), and Elsie Stephens (left). Ernest Stanford let the 1st Crawley Scouts meet at his Goffs Park home. The Pease Pottage campsite was named in his memory.

Children's party at Edwards. The volunteers who ran sports and social clubs, organizing events and encouraging participation by workers and their families, played a significant role in the New Town. There were parties for children in the community huts, in churches, and at union centres, as well as in factory canteens.

West Green Primary School's teddy bears' picnic, *c.* 1957. Miss Parr was thought to have made this delightful suggestion.

Mudlarks at Three Bridges, *c.* 1959. New and old residents called two local rivers The Mole. The New Town's water was piped from Weir Wood on the River Medway from September 1955. In case Monday washday and building needs in Three Bridges overtaxed previous supplies the Corporation's engineers instructed contractors to use water tanks, filled at the weekend.

Langley Green Junior School, *c.* 1968. It was the custom for class teachers to bring their own children to school when the annual class photograph was taken.

The fountain, Queens Square. If children seemed to be everywhere in Crawley so did bicycles. The birthrate reached twenty a week in the mid-1950s but the Cottage Hospital was still not replaced. The Regional Health Authority refused to build near the Hawth on a large site (which became Arden Road). Children were born at home or miles away.

West Green School band, 1960/1. Children played recorders and drums.

Langley Green School summer fête, 1966. This is one of Hephzibah Carman's photographs; she may be the shorter lady in the back row.

Northgate School sports day, 1952/3. Headmaster Mr Jones (left) has future Hazelwick teacher Thomas or Thompson on his left. Derek Ward holds the house sign and Pat Sims is on his left. Playing fields close to the schools were welcomed by Londoners.

Hazelwick School swimmers with Lorretta Ward holding the cup, *c*. 1954. When Crawley's pool was built Alec Haynes of Vitamins Ltd helped, for he had installed the filter system there. Vitamins Ltd allowed local children to use their pool after they had started sneaking into the grounds.

Brownies and guides, 13 October 1957. A representative of each east Crawley group at the dedication of colours, Christ Church, Worth Park Avenue.

May queen and attendants, 1960. Jean Dent (left, behind) and Olive Lott with May queen Linda Whitcombe, Susan Kemp (left) and Carol Pascoe at St Barnabas church, Pound Hill. Miss Lott was very active in Pound Hill and Three Bridges Brownies and Guides. She worked at the Corporation's Housing Office.

Langley Green Girl Guides, 1958/9. This group includes Maureen Hamblin (front left), Patricia Woodard (rear centre), and Zena Preston next to Jennifer Budden (front right).

Ron Prosser in the 4th Worth Scouts, *c.* 1950. As the town grew the scouts had many more troops. Ernest Stanford, a member of the Development Corporation, was keen on the movement. The 4th Worth's hut was ready in September 1954.

Thomas Bennett School presents *Our Town*, *c.* 1964. Seated, left to right: Paul Flindell, Richard Marshall, Christine Broomfield with Jenny Fairman behind, Pat Rudge with Carol Foster behind, Bob Lamont, Joan Cruddas, Christine Ward, Bill Brewer. Kneeling, centre: Stephen Pudephatt with Sue Mills on his left.

Girls' Nautical Training Corps, *c.* 1968. Pauline Woodard receives an award from Commander Blaxland. The corps (now Sea Cadets) was one of dozens of youth groups in the New Town.

Pound Hill Junior School off to camp, 1970. Standing, left to right: Wilhelmina Atkins, Susan Batch, Christopher Vaughan Williams, Peter Flinn, Gary Ryan, Steven Winbolt, Gay Fowler, Caroline Wagstaff, Sally Hoskin, Mr Hathaway, Dawn Pettingel, Donna Laban, Mr Burglass, Antony Knight, ? Channan, -?-, Gordon Laine, Stewart Austin, Robin Bond. Seated: Neil Marriott, Jane Stone, Susan Sinclair, Kay Brown, Andrew Spencer, Andrew Smith, Eric Freestone, Steven Heard, -?-, Sean O'Conner, Ian Johnson, Beverley Trusell, Gillian Wagstaff, Mark Roberts.

Building the pool at Hazelwick School.

Apprentices and a Prime Minister, *c.* 1972. Edward Heath's yacht *Morning Cloud* was modelled in stainless steel, brass and copper by A.P.V. apprentices who presented it to the Prime Minister at 10 Downing Street. Left to right: Madron Seligman, Roy Lane, training officer David Knight-Dewell, four apprentices, Johnny Hollick (in charge of the apprentice school from 1963), Les Derbyshire (superintendent coppersmith apprentices), Heath, machine-shop superintendent Peter Miller, Peter Seligman, apprentice.

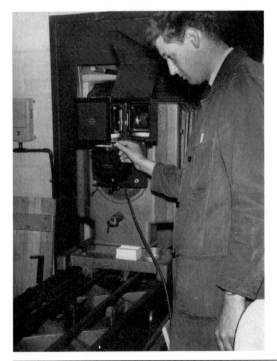

Hubners of Kelvin Way, lithographic printers. Ron Prosser was an apprentice at Hubners between 1954 and 1960, and here is studying a litho camera. Garrard and Lofthouse of Gatwick Road took over Hubners.

The staff at Crawley College of Further Education, 10 April 1956.

See page 159 for names.

Engineering apprentices, *c.* 1961. Apprentices signed on with local manufacturers for five years, getting practical experience on the shop floor and day release for studies. Crawley College's annexe, Spencers Road, was purchased by the Sikh community in 1981.

Apprentices at Bowthorpe, *c.* 1957. Bowthorpe house magazine named the first five apprentices as A.F. Green, M.B. Neary, C. Lay, T.M. Inman and T.B. Aylward.

SECTION TEN

People

Some people associated with Crawley had national and even international fame. A senior civil servant at the housing ministry in the 1940s was Harold Abrahams, whose 1920s athletic career became known to a later generation through the film Chariots of Fire.

Better known in 1949 was John George Haigh, who coaxed Olive Durand-Deacon from London to look over his so-called plastics factory. His West Green shed was examined by police who charged Haigh with murder. He thought he had destroyed the evidence but his victim was identified by her dentures. Development Corporation officials recall that some migrants asked to see where the acid bath murderer had been at work.

Hermits Road, Three Bridges, built in 1955, was named after Joe Kruger, a well-educated eccentric who had lived in a dug-out on farmland there. Crawley's hermit played chess and grew vegetables.

Sean Bourke taught morse code at Ifield Air Training Corps in the 1950s. Later he was in Wormwood Scrubs prison where he met Soviet spy George Blake. Bourke's radio skills helped Blake escape.

One Thomas Bennett School pupil became a Labour MP for Bristol. Others led less public lives.

Crawley Development Corporation comes to an end. Left to right: Bob Bryant (architect), S. Howgrave-Graham (chief architect), Bill Batty (accountant), Joyce Bell (administrator), Ken Todd (architect), Robin Clarke (chief executive), Tom Freeman (legal officer), Brian Roberts (engineer).

Annie Cheal, aged 98, 1976. Born in Ireland, she married Ernest Cheal whose family's nurseries had long been associated with Crawley.

Hazelwick School governors. Mrs Carman and A.P.V. works manager Robert May served Crawley in many fields.

Three Bridges Infants School, *c.* 1958. Standing, left to right: Mrs Watts, -?-, -?-, Mrs Patterson, -?-. Seated: -?-, -?-, Miss Scallard, Ivy Stobbart, Mrs Cox.

Part of the opening ceremony at Jordans Primary School, July 1959.

Percy Wales, parish councillor. He ran a corner shop where Ewhurst Road joined Ifield Road in West Green.

Grace Camfield, a leading Quaker. The Ifield meeting house has been a place of worship since 1676.

Camfield House, Ifield, opened in 1971. Quakers set out in 1967 to supply accommodation for up to twenty people who did not meet the rules other bodies had made.

Revd Charles Williams of Ifield did a great deal to help settlers make a good start in the New Town. He died in January 1973.

Jerzy Walerian Braun, Olympic medallist. One of the Polish people in Crawley, Braun was in the Second Army in Libya and Italy, and won seven Polish and three British war medals. He died in March 1968. His grave in Snell Hatch has the Olympic symbol, for he had won silver and bronze at Los Angeles in 1932. This is a wartime photograph.

Crawley parish councillors inspect Weir Wood reservoir. The River Medway was the New Town's source of water from 1955. A military pipeline from Balcombe to Tilgate, and a pre-stressed concrete tank at Pease Pottage then ceased to be used.

Piara Singh Tehara, 1963. Photographer and fingerprint expert in the Indian Police, he migrated to London in 1963 and found work at Monogram Electric Blankets, Gatwick Road. Trained as a television engineer, the then clean-shaven Sikh repaired televisions all over Crawley in the 1970s. Later workers from India also found jobs and sent for families when settled.

Sir Norman Longley opens Carman House. The contributions of Longley and Mrs Carman, both Old Towners, to Crawley New Town were substantial. Mrs Carman's typewritten memoirs are delightful.

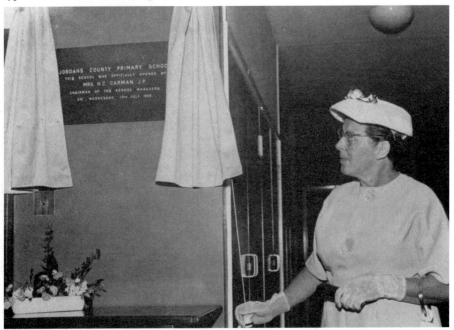

Hephzibah Carman, 1959. She was a school governor, a member of the parish council, a magistrate, and a staunch Labour Party member.

Vic Pellen, 1953. Schoolteacher and Tenants' Association leader, and active in socialist work from 1949, Pellen and his wife Jean were both educated in Horsham. Her support allowed him time to speak out for the underdog. Meetings with MPs and protests over rents developed from social affairs such as dances and outings to the coast.

Brenda Portwine at Lloyd's Register canteen, c. 1960. Right: E.W.J. Fenton. At first planners believed workers would live so close to the factories they would go home at midday. As companies relocated they were invited to use the canteens at A.P.V. and Edwards until their own were ready.

Her Majesty visits a New Town family, 1958. Kitty and Eric Hammond recall the police officer who checked their Ifield home for hidden photographers, for he opened a wardrobe and everything fell out, just 10 minutes before the visit. Later the RSPCA called to check reports that their dog had been locked up.

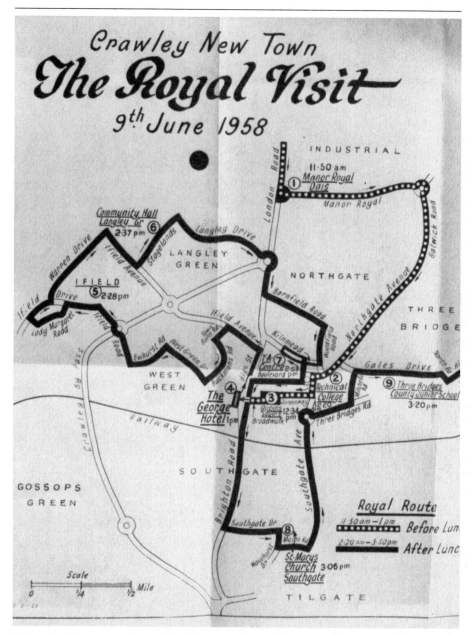

Crawley New Town
The Royal Visit
9th June 1958

When the Queen came some factories gave their staff time off. Four cine-cameras were hired by the amateur Crawley Film Unit.

Greeting the Queen, 1958. Reg Patrick (left) of the Corporation selected representatives from shops. Hazel Nesbitt of Leon's fashion shop presented a doll for Princess Anne. Reg was too nervous to use the camera he held.

Three Bridges Junior School, 1958. Many New Towners kept snaps and press cuttings of the day the Queen came to Crawley.

SECTION ELEVEN

Gatwick Airport

Although Silkin had spoken of the aviation industry when declaring Crawley-Three Bridges would be a new town, Gatwick aerodrome had no significance into the 1950s. Its railway station, however, was extremely useful for New Town workers and builders.

The airport was shut in 1956 and the road to London was diverted. Gatwick reopened in 1958. Charter and military subcontracting airlines then used Gatwick, which had a new station, too far to serve Crawley's industrial estate. The airport pulled workers from Crawley because uncertainties of industrial employment made craftsmen seek steadier work, and because aviation was a new business with fewer rules.

A single runway and noise were not problems as big-bodied jumbo jets came into use in the 1970s, and as more people used planes for holidays. The men and women who bravely moved thirty miles from London in the 1950s found their children were jetting off to the Mediterranean and other distant places. As they did, Crawley's industrial estate saw demolition contractors pulling down the Youngman, A.P.V., Sun d'Or, Brentford, Telcon, Stone, Duracell and Silentbloc factories.

Gatwick racecourse station. A Londoner who took a job in the New Town, travelling from Croydon, recalled that 'a stampede of men' poured off trains from London and rushed to Manor Royal in the 1950s. The closure of the station annoyed those who travelled to work in Crawley, for the airport station was too far north for comfort. Jack Bowthorpe suggested it should be kept open as a halt.

Crawley railway station, August 1968. The level crossing was not so easy to remove. It was the age of the motor car now, but the New Town employers were isolated on the industrial estate which had no station after Gatwick was redesigned.

British European Airways at Gatwick, *c. 1959*. Thomas Bennett was distressed when the small aerodrome was designated London's second airport as he thought it would destroy Crawley's economic base.

The November veteran car race. The airport roads provided a good viewing spot for the Old Crocks Race.

Gatwick Airport had regular railway trains to central London. The motorway link roads were omens of the future, when the fields (top) would become car parks.

NORTH APRON AND MAIN BUILDING, GATWICK AIRPORT

Gatwick Airport, *c.* 1960. Rebuilt and opened in 1958, the airport attracted local workers and led to labour shortages in Crawley. It cost sixpence to wander here, observing planes and travellers.

Crawley Development Corporation, 1948. (See page 20)

1	Colonel Charles Turner
2	Robert Jardine-Brown
3	Allwyn Sheppard-Fidler
4	Arthur McIntosh
5	Bryan Richards
6	Wilfred Bailey
7	Anthony Minoprio (consultant: designer of Crawley New Town)
8	Bill Batty
9	Jack Mercer
10	Mary Adams
11	Raymond Illsley
12	Gertie Martin
13	? Wright
14	Susan Tidbury
15	'Dicky' Bird
16	Mollie Dean
17	Ray Caplen
18	Tom Freeman
19	Muriel Legge
20	Robin Clarke
21	Geoff Cramp
22	Brian Roberts
23	Morris Milne
24	Ann Sturge
25	Pat Bluck
26	Kate Shelley
27	Sydney Napper
28	Bob Bryant
29	Nelson Foley
30	Ken Todd
31	Vic Land-Reeves
32	Stuart Howgrave-Graham
33	Joyce Bell
34	Mike Taunton
35	Elaine Randall
36	Joy Catt
37	Melody Dayrell
38	Jean Wright
39	Edward Cage
40	Betty Richardson
41	Arthur Dodd
42	Bernard Hunter
43	Stanley Brown
44	Wynn Thomas
45	Peter Swan
46	unknown
47	Michael Bourne
48	James Hartley
49	Roger Davis

Crawley College of Further Education, 1956. (See page 141)

1	T. Siklos
2	H. Gordon
3	W. Wade
4	L. Smith
5	W. Wales
6	E. White
7	O. Brown
8	T. Bailey
9	M. Dorkis
10	M. Helm
11	B. Turner
12	B. Chantler
13	M. Pearson
14	E. Sutton
15	E. Covey
16	O. Richardson
17	K. Jack
18	D. Kitchener
19	P. Bean
20	J. Monaghan
21	E. Sands
22	E. Small
23	M. Tait
24	A. Hazel
25	J. Hodgson
26	A. Bolding
27	T. Holt
28	G. Cone
29	R. Mitchell
30	C. Price
31	J. Wood
32	D. Waddling
33	C. Hughes
34	N. Tootill
35	J. Kendall
36	D. Roskilly
37	R. Thornton
38	F. Cooper
39	C. Branch
40	J. Carman
41	G. Robinson
42	M. Lord
43	S. Smith
44	J. Lendon
45	W. MacNamee
46	G. Spencer
47	E. Jones
48	L. Williams
49	I. Tanner
50	V. Evans
51	A. Mileham
52	H. Heisler
53	J. Nayler
54	D. Philcox
55	F. Holt
56	S. Holland
57	H. Maynard
58	G. Brown
59	W. Whittaker
60	W. Hitchcock
61	R. Sinden
62	R. Kelly
63	A. Lane
64	R. Maddocks
65	E. Harvey
66	R. Webster
67	E. Stanley
68	B. Mulqueen
69	–
70	A. Flegg
71	? Sewell
72	D. Hilliard
73	M. Bryson
74	K. Lowe
75	E. Barr
76	E. Pilcher
77	K. Wittey
78	J. Smith
79	J. Blanch
80	G. Kingshott
81	D. Daynes
82	T. Holmes
83	W. Impey
84	J. Jeffries
85	A. Owthwaite
86	A. Howell
87	E. Wansell
88	R. Stephens
89	L. Garrett
90	D. Mountford
91	J. Graham
92	E. Adams
93	P. Hipkiss
94	J. Chapman
95	J. Barnes

Acknowledgements

Patricia Allen • Sylvia & Vic Baker • John Baldry
John Baldwin & Bernard Barker (Three Bridges Cricket Club) • Tony Barnes
Arthur Bell • Peter Bennett • Audrey & Charles Bingham
Kazimierz Bortkiewicz (Polish Ex-Combatants Association of Great Britain)
Roy Brackpool • Oliver Brown • Andrew Brzezina • Frederick Carpenter
Brian Champion • Ron Chenapa • Robin Clarke
Don Clements (7th Crawley Scouts)
Marguerite & David Clifford • Ivan Clout • Val Cooper • Edna & Len Covey
Bert Crane • *Crawley Observer* • Peter Crosskey
Croydon Local Studies Library • Tony Danser • Nigel Dennis • Mario Dezzani
Phil Edney • Vera Ellmers • Alf Ells • Pauline Emsley • Elsie Finch
Betty & Gordon Flint • Frank Fowler (Edwards High Vacuum) • Eric Freestone
Brenda & Ron Frei • Charlie Frost • Joyce & Pete Fry • Fiona Graham
Margaret Graham • Greater London Record Office • Maureen Green
Kitty & Eric Hammond • Colin Heaysman • Derek Hicks • John Hicks
Peter Hillier • Lilian & Ron Hofmann • Johnny Hollick
Barbara & Fred Hollingdale • Lois Huntley • Pamela Jacob • Irene & Les James
Gary Jennings (Smith Kline Beecham) • Vernon Jones • Charles Kay
Vic Lawton • Carrie & Tony Leader • Don Lee • Harry Lindsey
Ray Lloyd (Crawley Rugby Football Club) • Norman Longley • Olive Lott
Reg Meadus • Brian Moore • Brenda Morgan • May Musselwhite
National Westminster Bank • Edward O'Brien • Paul Oliver • Christine Owen
Leslie Parsons • Ray Parsons • Lynn Patrick • Reg Patrick • Charlie Peace
Ian Pegg • Vic Pellen • Elsie & Jack Perkins • David Polhill • Ron Prosser
Brian Pryke • Public Record Office • Robert Randall • Brian Roberts
Stella Robinson • Royal Institute of British Architects • Howard Rye
Win Sampson • Ken Saunders • Mary Smith • Maureen & David Stanton
Jean & Jim Steele • Ivy Stobbart • Colleen Sullivan
Sussex Racial Equality Council • Mike Syrett • Tony Syrett • Ken Tamon
Piara Singh Tehara • Three Bridges Wives Group • Fran & Bernard Tolan
Audrey & Bernie Vaux • Dave Vincent (Vent-Axia) • June Wakefield
Derek Ward • Norma & Olga Ward • Stan Ward • Renate Warner • Jim Warren
Arthur Welch • West Sussex Record Office
West Sussex County Council Library Service
Anne Wheeldon (Hammersmith & Fulham Archives & Local History Centre)
Jack Williams • Pam & Tony Wright • Dave Young

The enthusiasm of Les James enabled us to make contacts that were very
fruitful. Peter Crosskey copied worn photographs with skill.